A BOOK OF
Promises

Elizabeth Laird ◻ *Illustrated by Michael Frith*

A DK INK BOOK
DK PUBLISHING, INC.

The world is big out there, little one,
so put your hand in mine.

When you are hungry,
I will feed you.

If you're cold, I will warm you.

If you're sick, I will nurse you.

And if you meet with trouble, big or small,
I'll stand by you, come what may.

When you speak,
I will listen.

When you offer me gifts,
I will thank you.

When you do well, I will praise you.

If perils and dangers come near you,
I'll stand by your side
and battle them away.

And if you're scared of a nameless fear,
I'll hold you in my arms and protect you.

*I promise that I will
never harm you,
or threaten you,
or frighten you.*

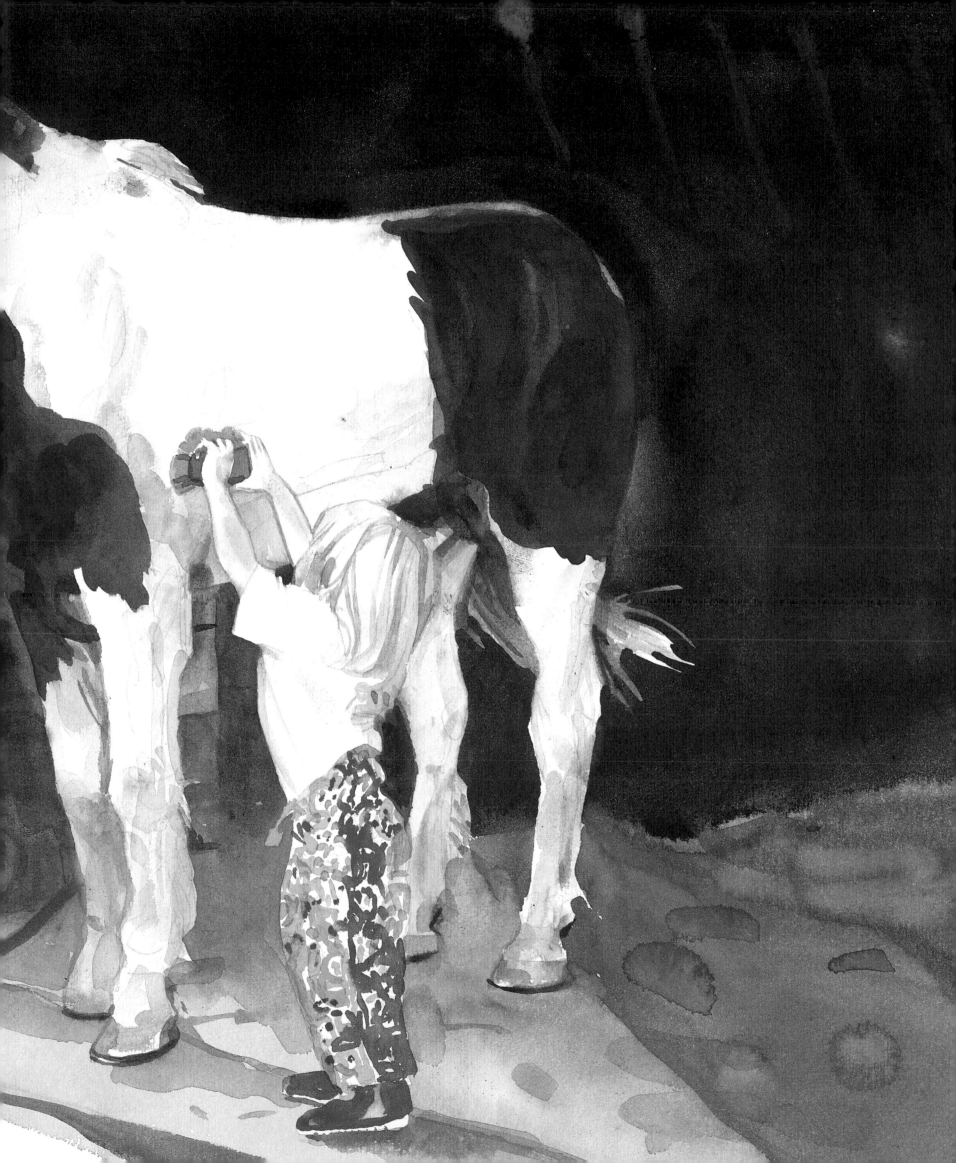

And if you should ever do me wrong,
I'll try my best to forgive you.

When you're sad,
I'll cry with you.
When you're happy,
I'll laugh with you.

I'll show you where beauty is,
and we'll walk there together.

And when all the promises are made,
there's still one more.
I promise that I'll love you,
whatever may befall.

For Molly
E.L.
For Frieda
M.F.

DK Publishing, Inc.
95 Madison Avenue
New York, New York 10016

www.dk.com

Library of Congress Cataloging-in-Publication Data
Laird, Elizabeth
A book of promises/Elizabeth Laird;illustrated by Michael Frith. — 1st ed.
p. cm.
"A DK Ink book."
Summary: A parent promises to love and care for a child in every situation.
ISBN 0-7894-2547-5
[1. Promises—Fiction. 2. Parent and child—Fiction.]
I. Frith, Michael K.,ill. II. Title.
PZ7.L1579 Bo 2000 [E]—dc21 99-31531 CIP

The illustrations for this book were painted in watercolor.
The text of this book is set in 29 point Stempel Garamond Italic.
Printed and bound in Spain
D.L. TO: 167-2000

First Edition, 2000
2 4 6 8 10 9 7 5 3